GRAPHIC HISTORY

THE STORY OF

Jamestown

by Eric Braun
illustrated by Steve Erwin,
Keith Williams, and Charles Barnett III

Consultant:
Crandall A. Shifflett, Professor of History
Virginia Tech
Blacksburg, Virginia

Capstone
press

North Mankato, Minnesota

Graphic Library is published by Capstone Press,
1710 Roe Crest Drive, North Mankato, Minnesota 56003.
www.capstonepub.com

Library of Congress Cataloging-in-Publication Data
Braun, Eric, 1971–
    The story of Jamestown / by Eric Braun; illustrated by Steve Erwin, Keith Williams, and
Charles Barnett III.
    p. cm.—(Graphic library. Graphic history)
    Includes bibliographical references and index.
    ISBN-13: 978-0-7368-4967-8 (hardcover)   ISBN-10: 0-7368-4967-X (hardcover)
    ISBN-13: 978-0-7368-6210-3 (softcover pbk.)   ISBN-10: 0-7368-6210-2 (softcover pbk.)
    1. Jamestown (Va.)—History—Juvenile literature. I. Erwin, Steve, ill. II. Williams, Keith, ill.
III. Barnett, Charles, III, ill. IV. Title. V. Series.
F234.J3B69 2006
975.5'4251—dc22   2005013592

Summary: In graphic novel format, tells the story of Jamestown, the first permanent English
settlement in North America.

Art and Editorial Direction
Jason Knudson and Blake A. Hoena

Designers
Bob Lentz and Juliette Peters

Colorist
Ben Hunzeker

Editor
Donald Lemke

Editor's note: Direct quotations from primary sources are indicated by a yellow background.

Direct quotations appear on the following pages:
Pages 17, 25 (all), from *Love and Hate in Jamestown: John Smith, Pocahontas, and the Heart of
    a New Nation* by David A. Price (New York: Knopf, 2003).

Printed in the United States of America in North Mankato, Minnesota.
042018   000027

Table of Contents

CHAPTER 1

In Honor of Our King

During the 1500s, Spain and Portugal gained great riches from their colonies in South America. Hoping to find similar success, England sent explorers to North America. In 1606, King James I gave a group called the London Company permission to settle a new colony.

In December, 108 men set sail aboard three ships, the *Susan Constant*, the *Godspeed*, and the *Discovery*.

The explorers dreamed of finding gold and a route to the Pacific Ocean.

A few days later, Chief Wowinchopunk arrived with a deer and 100 armed Paspahegh Indians.

Defend yourselves!

No! Don't shoot.

They come in peace.

Many settlers believed the Indians wanted to fight and scared them off. Afterwards, Wingfield locked all the settlers' guns on the ship. He wanted to handle things peacefully.

Meanwhile, Newport prepared to explore the area north of Jamestown. On May 21, he set out on the James River with 23 men, including Smith.

I will return soon with gold and other riches of this land.

We should find food and build shelter—not waste our time searching for gold.

9

In early 1608, Newport and Wingfield sailed from Jamestown. Days later another ship, the *Phoenix*, arrived.

Food!

The settlers of Jamestown lived through spring on the ship's supplies.

They also received goods from helpful Indians.

Thank you for bringing us more food, Pocahontas.

Now we all owe you our lives.

With Wingfield gone, the settlers decided Smith was their best leader. They made him president.

As of today, there's a new law around here.

He that will not work shall not eat.

17

CHAPTER 3

A Struggle to Survive

Under Smith's strict leadership, the settlers of Jamestown worked hard and survived. In August of 1609, more ships arrived. They brought women and children to the colony, as well as news from London.

A new governor will arrive soon.

Jamestown no longer needs a president, Smith.

Until he arrives, I'm still in charge here!

With Smith gone, Jamestown needed a leader. The settlers chose George Percy, an educated gentleman from a noble family.

We have at most three months of food left, President Percy.

And our fishing nets have rotted in the water.

Ratcliffe, tell this Powhatan to give us more food.

Percy's demands for food angered Powhatan. The chief sent men to attack the settlers.

They forced the settlers to stay inside the fort.

We're trapped!

What will we eat?

That winter became known as the "starving time."

Chief Powhatan wouldn't trade with West. So, West attacked Powhatan's villages. During an attack in 1613, the English captured Pocahontas.

Look, we've caught Powhatan's daughter.

Take her back to Jamestown as our prisoner.

Even as fights continued with American Indians, the London Company wanted the colony to make money. A colonist named John Rolfe soon had the answer.

This tobacco from the West Indies grows well here.

It's sweeter than what the English are used to smoking. I bet they'd buy it.

CHAPTER 4

The End of Jamestown

A year after being captured, Pocahontas continued to live in Jamestown. While there, she learned the English language and religion.

As Rolfe's tobacco profits grew, so did his love for Powhatan's daughter. In April 1614, Rolfe married Pocahontas. Their marriage created a peace between Powhatan Indians and the colonists.

John, I notice more English have been coming to Jamestown.

Yes, dear. They come to grow tobacco. It has proven very popular back in England.

With the success of Rolfe's tobacco, smaller towns started growing around Jamestown. Soon, Jamestown became the capital of the Virginia Colony.

In 1619, settlers created a general assembly, known as the House of Burgesses. This government body made laws for the colony.

Be it enacted that no injury or oppression be wrought by the English against the Indians.

Peace with the Indians will only work if both sides agree.

A year earlier, Chief Powhatan had died. His brother, Opechancanough, became the new Powhatan chief. Opechancanough made a promise to the English.

We will not break the peace between us.

The sky should sooner fall.

Jamestown

✳ Jamestown is known as the first permanent English settlement in North America. But more than 30 years earlier, Englishmen settled on Roanoke Island, off the North Carolina coast. Today, Roanoke is called the Lost Colony. No one knows what happened to these settlers.

✳ In 1616, John Rolfe, Pocahontas, and their baby traveled to London. Less than a year later, Pocahontas died at the age of 22. Some historians believe she died of pneumonia or tuberculosis caused by the city's foul, smoky air.

✳ After returning to England, Captain John Smith recovered from his injury. Smith never returned to Jamestown. But in April 1614, he traveled to the areas of Maine and Massachusetts Bay. Smith named this region New England.

✳ In 1624, Smith wrote a book about his experiences at Jamestown. In the book, Smith claims that Pocahontas saved him from being killed by Chief Powhatan. Most historians believe Powhatan never wanted to kill Smith. Instead, they think either Pocahontas was performing an American Indian ceremony, or Smith made up the story.

In August 1619, the first Africans came to North America aboard a Dutch ship. The 20 or so men were sold in Jamestown for food and supplies. Eventually, thousands of other Africans would be shipped to America as slaves.

In 1676, a young planter named Nathaniel Bacon led a revolt against Jamestown's governor, William Berkeley. Bacon believed Berkeley could have stopped Indian attacks on settlements west of Jamestown. During what is known as Bacon's Rebellion, most of Jamestown burned to the ground.

In 1994, archaeologists from the Association for Preservation of Virginia Antiquities (APVA) started digging in the area of Jamestown. They found two of the three walls from the fort. They also found thousands of artifacts from the time of the first settlers. Today, the area of Jamestown is a national historic site.

GLOSSARY

archaeologist (ar-kee-OL-uh-jist)—a scientist who studies objects from long ago

artifact (ART-uh-fakt)—an object made by human beings, especially a tool or weapon used in the past

charter (CHAR-tur)—a formal document that states the duties and rights of a group of people

confederacy (kuhn-FED-ur-uh-see)—a union of groups; Powhatan groups united under one government called the Powhatan Confederacy.

territory (TER-uh-tor-ee)—a large area of land

INTERNET SITES

FactHound offers a safe, fun way to find Internet sites related to this book. All of the sites on FactHound have been researched by our staff.

Here's how:

1. Visit *www.facthound.com*
2. Type in this special code **073684967X** for age-appropriate sites. Or enter a search word related to this book for a more general search.
3. Click on the **Fetch It** button.

FactHound will fetch the best sites for you!

READ MORE

Doak, Robin S. *Smith: John Smith and the Settlement of Jamestown*. Exploring the World. Minneapolis: Compass Point Books, 2003.

Riehecky, Janet. *The Settling of Jamestown*. Landmark Events in American History. Milwaukee: World Almanac Library, 2002.

Sonneborn, Liz. *Pocahontas, 1595–1617*. American Indian Biographies. Mankato, Minn.: Blue Earth Books, 2003.

BIBLIOGRAPHY

Barbour, Philip L. *Pocahontas and Her World*. Boston: Houghton Mifflin, 1970.

Bridenbaugh, Carl. *Jamestown: 1544–1699*. New York: Oxford University Press, 1980.

Price, David A. *Love and Hate in Jamestown: John Smith, Pocahontas, and the Heart of a New Nation*. New York: Knopf, 2003.

Rountree, Helen C. *Pocahontas, Powhatan, Opechancanough: Three Indian Lives Changed by Jamestown*. Charlottesville: University of Virginia Press, 2005.

INDEX